MW01591448

Campfire
Publishing

Jekyll Says ...

Good Things Cats Do, That You Should, Too!

D.C. Blackbird

Jekyll Says...
Good Deeds Cats Do, That You Should, Too!

by
D.C. Blackbird

This book was written for my feline companion named Jekyll. The characters, incidents, and dialogues were inspired by Jekyll and other companion cats in our home, or are the products of the author's imagination. Any resemblance to actual events, or locales, or persons, or felines, in Kittyland or Humanland, or cats outside of our home, is entirely coincidental.

Profits from the sale of this book benefit animal adoption, care, liberation, rescue, and welfare organizations. If you know of any such organizations that would like to sell this book as part of its fundraising efforts, please contact the Publisher at **WelcomeToKittyland.com.**

Jekyll Illustrations by Christine P. Flores

Graphic Design by Leah Frieday

Dedication

"Jekyll Says ..." is dedicated to all the non-human animals who have ever been eaten, harmed, hunted, murdered, and/or tortured anywhere, anytime, around the world, throughout history.

This book is specifically dedicated to Jekyll, Radar, Autumn, Smudge, Gizmo, Jasper, Annabelle, Double-Stuff, Buddy, and of course their Human Mom who loved Jekyll more than the words in this book, or any other, can fully express.

Table of Contents

Foreword

My name is Jekyll. I was born in North Carolina in 1999. I was found as a baby in a dirty ditch because no one wanted me. Even though I was really small, and adorable, and at the time I even had bright blue eyes as baby kitties like me tend to have. It is difficult to believe that I was abandoned on the side of the road as if I was worthless garbage. How could anyone treat another living being like that? Especially when one notices the unique marking on my face. Everyone knows that a special marking means great things await those who have them. A marking like mine meant that I was destined to be blessed with good fortune and would develop miraculous skills, talents, and gifts. Without a doubt, I was favored to have a treasure trove of happy and wondrous days. After all, many of the great heroes of mythology and folklore had birthmarks or special markings. Clearly, good fortune awaited me!

As was preordained, two wonderful Humans took me into their home. I was brushed off, freshened up, my trusty tuxedo was cleaned, and I was given boodles of food, water, and love. They raised me in a fun and affectionate household. When I first arrived, I had the best big brother (Radar) and sister (Autumn) that anyone could want! And soon I had many more! What a wonderful family! We were always singing and dancing and playing! With their endless affection, encouragement, and support, I was able to follow my dreams and become all I was destined be. Boy, oh, boy! Whoever threw me away really missed out! And you are missing out, too, unless you go to a shelter and adopt a homeless cat or dog. Even if you already have one or two (like my Humans did), perhaps you can find it in your heart to take in another, and give him or her a loving home. They need you.

I supervised the writing and publication of this book so I could share with you some of the tips that helped me become the envy of kitties everywhere on earth and in Kittyland. Please read the following poems slow, and aloud, so they sound best. Whether you are a Kitty, Doggie, Furry Critter, or a Human—if you follow my simple tips, you can be happy, healthier, and successful, too!

Paws, Purrs, Licks, & Kisses!

Jekyll 🐾🐾

Do the Things I Say

Jekyll says, "Do the things I say."
All through the night and through the day.
I know about life. Yes, it's true.
My cat wisdom, I'll share with you.

I'm super clean, and dress real well.
My words are clear, just like a bell.
I'll tell you things you ought to know.
To be happy and not feel low.

Hey all you babies—listen now!
You'll be awesome! I'll show you how.
If you're a kid — take my advice.
Listen up! Become super nice.

If you're grown up, then listen in.
Want to be great? You'll get my spin.
So read my book. Let's make a deal.
I'll show you how to think and feel.

Just be all eyes, and be all ears.
Afraid to change? I'll ease your fears.
You might think I'm a Know-it-all.
Well, you'd be right! Let's have a ball!

Got collywobbles inside you?
Stick with me, friend. I'll see you through!
Feeling at the end of the rope?
Well, don't worry. I'm here with hope.

So what if you're an Average Joe?
Please don't be a couch potato!
When you look back upon your days.
You'll think, "Jekyll showed me the ways!"

GOOD DEEDS
CATS DO,
THAT YOU SHOULD,
TOO!

Wake Up Happy!

Jekyll says to, "Wake up happy."
Up and about! Make it snappy!
It's your day, so be nice and bright.
Make choices that you know are right.

Find the time for breakfast in bed.
Don't let clutter fill up your head.
Refresh yourself with fresh-squeezed juice.
Put on some music and cut loose!

Do jumping jacks. Don't be a schlep.
Strut outdoors with pep in your step.
Waking up happy is the way.
For you to start your greatest day!

Eat Healthy Meals!

Jekyll says to, "Eat healthy meals."
Gobble up goodies. Spin your wheels.
You'll get a healthy, shiny coat.
And energy to row a boat!

Eat lots of veggies and some fruit.
They're great treasures and priceless loot!
Learn all you can about your food.
Pigs and birds don't want to be chewed.

Eat food from gardens and the trees.
And no wiggly things from the seas.
You can get protein anyhow.
So there's no need to eat a cow.

All animals found on a farm.
Just want your love and don't want harm.
You can eat healthy — starting now.
Eat your veggies and say, "me-wow!"

Be Clean!

Jekyll says, "Make sure you are clean."
And be the freshest on the scene!
Splishin' and Splashin' — Baths are fun.
Be as bright as the shining sun!

Sing in the tub — giggle and laugh.
Put some soapy suds in your bath.
Be so clean that others will stare.
Treat your body with utmost care!

Get squeaky clean each day and night.
Lather up and you'll smell all right.
Don't think that this is all hogwash.
Scrub real well and you'll look real posh!

Dress Your Best!

Jekyll says, "Always dress your best."
Set an example for the rest.
Clean pants! Clean shirts! Clean underwear!
If you don't have them—don't despair!

Pop clothes in the washing machine.
Your threads look best when they are clean!
Dress up to the nines when you can.
Make sure to look all spic and span.

You should look dainty or dapper.
Be like candy in the wrapper!
Spruce up your look and be in bloom.
You will be the toast of the room.

Always put on fresh socks and shoes.
Dress as if you'll be on the news.
So take good care of what you wear.
And don't forget to comb your hair!

Make Others Smile!

Jekyll says to, "Make others smile."
Start a trend with your happy style.
Smile at people who you don't know.
Seeds of happiness you will sow.

A smile that's true shines shiny bright.
And seen by all each day or night!
Treat people gently and with care.
There's good in people everywhere.

So go and smile willy-nilly.
Do not worry. It's not silly.
Smiles are free so give them away.
You can do it—starting today!

Be a Hard Worker!

Jekyll says, "Work hard and be great."
Arrive early and don't be late.
Don't ever be a lazy loon!
Work all day and take lunch at noon.

When you can, be part of a team.
Sharing credit should be the theme.
Let others know that you're a whiz.
With all you know about your biz.

Do your best and love what you do.
Be good and proud and smart and true.
Remember what all wise cats say.
And you'll love your work every day.

Shake Your Booty!

It's a song!
So sing along!

Jekyll says, "Shake your booty now!"
No need for me to show you how.
For all good reasons you should dance!
Shake around in your fancy pants.

Start shaking your tail in the air.
Shake it! Shake it! With lots of flair!
Are others watching? Maybe so!
Set an example! Lead the show!

This isn't just some gibberish.
Wiggle your tail like licorice.
Jekyll says, "Shake your booty now!"
Shake it! Shake it! And sing, "MEOW!!!"

Learn New Things!

Jekyll says, "Always learn new things."
Smart people aren't ding-a-lings.
Learn to paint or to write a book.
Yes, it's high time to learn to cook!

Only lazy folks do nothing.
And their heads are filled with stuffing.
Broaden horizons. Learn things new.
Remember to be true to you.

Be Someone's Hero!

Jekyll says, "Be someone's hero."
And you'll never be a zero.
No need for outfits or some capes.
Don't get in any kinds of scrapes.

Defend the helpless all the time.
Help those in need and heed this rhyme.
Be brave, be strong, and be your best.
Stand up! Put bullies to the test!

Don't ever start a donnybrook.
But when you're needed—take a look.
Let others know you're not afraid.
To help all those in need of aid.

Note: "Donnybrook" is Irish slang for a public quarrel, dispute, or, brawl.

Be Proud of
Who You Are!

Always be proud of who you are.
Jekyll says that makes you a star!
Your nice smile and your golden heart.
Are treasures that set you apart.

Show your true self for all to see.
Your greatest treasures are for free.
Only you can choose your value—
So shine like gold in every hue!

Get Plenty of Rest

Jekyll says, "Get plenty of rest."
Staying up late is not the best.
Catch lots of Z'zzz in a warm place.
Relax your body and your face.

Settle your tongue. Unclench your jaw.
Unwind your tail. Recline your paw.
Imagine you're floating down stream.
Close your eyes and begin to dream ...

Afterword

The central motivation to write this book was to immortalize Jekyll. We did not want him to be forgotten. He deserves more than that. He was special and there are lessons that cats and humans can learn from the fine examples he set in his extraordinary life.

Jekyll left Humanland on June 9, 2011 in order to return to Kittyland where his skills and abilities were certainly needed. We miss him so much and we think about him every day, but we know that no friend or companion, no matter what type they are, stays in Humanland as long as any of us want them to. But we were fortunate to have known him for as long as we have. I don't know what our lives would have been like without Jekyll, but I know that we have been enriched by his presence. We can honestly say that Jekyll was quite unlike other kitties. The "stories" in this book are subjects that epitomized Jekyll's personality. He woke up happy, he loved to be clean, he made others smile, he showed up at our home office every day and was prepared to "work", he was a "Hero," he cared for those he loved, he was proud of who he was, and everything else that you have read about in this book. And yes, he honestly DID shake his booty! We learned so much from Jekyll, as have others. Now it is your turn. Please spend your life doing the things that "Jekyll Says ..."

In addition, if you can find it in your heart, please immediately travel to any kill shelter and adopt a homeless cat or dog and give him or her a loving home. You can do it.

Equally as important, please make the effort to adopt a vegan diet. It will be better for the environment, and it will be healthy for your body and mind. Understand this: Doing so will save the lives of thousands of innocent animals over the course of your lifetime.

The world will be a better place if you and others do the above. You can do it. Believe me.

D.C. Blackbird

About

About Jekyll

Jekyll began his career as a well-respected Supervisor in his Human's kitchen (when meals were being prepared). His attention to detail won him much praise from family and friends, and he was soon promoted to supervise his Humans in other endeavors throughout each and every room of their home. In the home office, he offered his unique perspective and invaluable advice to his Human Dad concerning important business decisions. Jekyll also contributed immensely to creative endeavors that his Human parents engaged in.

Currently, Jekyll is a well-respected professor of Catology and Humanology at Feline University in Kittyland, where he shares his extensive knowledge and valuable experience and all the important things that he learned while he visited Humanland.

About D.C. Blackbird

D.C. Blackbird is an American poet, songwriter, and author. D.C. is an advocate of animal adoption, care, liberation, rescue, rights, and welfare, as well as a proponent of Veganism. D.C. works closely with domestic and farm animals, and wildlife around the world, and is dedicated to telling stories about their experiences and adventures in Humanland, as well as their own Homelands.

About the Illustrator

Christine P. Flores is an Illustrator and Cartoonist. She loves and takes care of a special and beautiful blind cat named Bubux.

About the Graphic Designer

Leah Frieday is a creative designer with a full-sized furry and feather family. Her home is filled with great love from their weiner dog, Chanel, the 'Big Baby', Toupi and Binou, the kitty sisters, and Kiki the Cockatiel. All of her furry babies were found or were adopted. Rebecca, is Leah's daughter and she looks forward to a life of caring for, and protecting all precious beings in the animal kingdom.

Are you ready to learn even more from Jekyll and about Kittyland? Please stay tuned, because more books and poems are coming your way. You and your friends can order:

"**Jekyll Says ...**" and "**Jekyll Says More!**" and "**Dreaming of Kittyland!**"

and other books from D.C. Blackbird from the same place you ordered this book.

Jekyll Says ... visit **WelcomeToKittyland.com**

Campfire
Publishing

37488758R00022